P Gauguin.

THE LIFE AND WORKS OF

GAUGUIN

Douglas Mannering

A Compilation of Works from the
BRIDGEMAN ART LIBRARY

PARRAGON

Gauguin

This edition first published in Great Britain in 1994
by Parragon Book Service Limited

© 1994 Parragon Book Service Limited

ISBN 1 85813 526 5

Printed in Italy

Designer: Robert Mathias

IN THE CASE OF PAUL GAUGUIN the cliché is accurate: he became a legend in his own lifetime. After his death, novels and films sustained the legend, and there can be few people who have not heard of the stockbroker who sacrificed everything to an overmastering urge to paint, eventually renouncing civilization and ending his life in a tropical paradise. For once, the legend is not too far from the truth, though its rough edges have been smoothed out – a process which began with the writings of Gauguin, himself an adept at self-promotion.

Gauguin was born in Paris on 7 June 1848. When he was a year old, his father, a political journalist, embarked with his family for Peru, but died on the voyage. However, thanks to his mother's wealthy connections in Lima, Gauguin spent his first seven years there in comfort before the family returned to France in 1855. At the age of 17, Paul joined the merchant marine. In his five years at sea he rose to second lieutenant and visited Panama and the Pacific, the tropical places that would always haunt his imagination.

In 1871 Gauguin returned to Paris, where an influential family friend found him a job with a stockbroker. He spent the next decade as a successful and respectable businessman and husband, marrying a Danish girl, Mette Sophie Gad, by whom he had five children.

Early in the 1870s Gauguin became an enthusiastic

'Sunday painter', and by 1876 he was proficient enough to have a landscape accepted for exhibition at the annual official Salon. But he soon preferred to exhibit with the Impressionists, who were still widely regarded as outrageous rebels. Working hard during his free time, Gauguin adopted the Impressionist technique of painting landscapes on the spot, using small brushstrokes of pure colour to capture atmospheric effects. Like his great contemporaries Cézanne and Van Gogh, he found Impressionism liberating, although he would eventually forge a very different style.

Gauguin undoubtedly wanted to retire from business and become a professional painter. What is less clear is whether he would have done so if there had not been an economic collapse in 1882; at the very least, his financial reverses gave him the excuse he needed to begin a new career, at the age of 35, as a full-time artist.

Years of hardship followed. Mette took refuge with her family in Copenhagen, joined for a time by Gauguin. After he left, they never lived together again. In 1887 Gauguin made his first artistic excursion into the tropics, spending a few months in Panama and Martinique. Driven back to France by malaria and poverty, he returned with canvases alive with newly liberated colour.

However, Gauguin's artistic progress was even more striking during his visits in the late 1880s to Britanny, then still remote and stimulatingly 'primitive'. There he began to develop his distinctive style, with its simplified, boldly outlined forms and strong colours. It was largely formed by 1888, when he spent a disastrous two months at Arles with Vincent van Gogh.

By 1891 Gauguin was established as a leading figure among the artists and poets of Paris. But, still miserably poor, he made the extraordinary decision to settle in faraway Tahiti. The most celebrated of all his paintings were done on the island, and these images of an uncorrupted primitive simplicity have had an enduring impact on the Western imagination. But although Gauguin did love the tropics, life remained hard, and by 1893 he was back in Paris, hoping that his Tahitian canvases would create a sensation and bring him fame and security at last.

Towards the end of a disappointing two years, Gauguin returned to Tahiti. He was now a sick man, with illnesses aggravated by an undiagnosed syphilitic condition. In and out of hospital, sometimes doing menial jobs and sometimes caught up in local politics and journalism, his artistic output was irregular, yet during this period he produced some of his greatest works.

In 1901 Gauguin made his final flight from encroaching civilization, settling in the Marquesas. His pleasure in his new paradise was quickly undermined by serious conflicts with the local authorities, and he was still appealing against a three-month prison sentence for libel when his turbulent life was ended by a heart attack on 8 May 1903.

▷ **The Painter's Family in the Garden** c.1881-2

Oil on canvas

INTENTIONALLY OR OTHERWISE, in this picture Gauguin has put forward an idyllic view of solid, prosperous family life. The setting is the garden of a large, comfortable house in the rue Carcel in Paris, where Gauguin's financial success made it possible for him to keep his family in some style. At this point in his career he had been gainfully employed for almost a decade, having apparently put behind him his roving years in the merchant navy. He had also progressed in art from the status of a gifted amateur to that of a fellow-colleague, still not a full-time professional but accepted by most of the Impressionists with whom he showed his works. But although Gauguin devoted more and more of his free time to art, we cannot be sure that he would ever have risked the pleasant existence pictured here by giving up his business career had fate not taken a hand.

◁ **Snow Scene** 1883

Oil on canvas

IN 1882 THE FRENCH stock market collapsed. Gauguin suffered heavy losses and found himself out of a job. If there was any possibility of his re-establishing himself, he chose not to pursue it, taking the opportunity to embrace the life of an artist. His statement that, 'From now on I shall paint every day' highlights the constraints under which he had worked during his ten years as a 'Sunday painter'. His early works reveal the tension between Impressionism – painting landscapes out of doors, to capture the fleeting atmosphere – and the composed, figure-oriented style to which his temperament was more attracted. *Snow Scene* is Gauguin at his most Impressionist; the subject was frequently tackled by Pissarro, Monet and Sisley. Like them, however, Gauguin jibbed at the prospect of painting his way to pneumonia and compromised by making an oil sketch in the open and then painting the final picture in his studio.

△ **The Beach at Dieppe** 1885

Oil on canvas

IN NOVEMBER 1884, having failed to make a living as an artist in Paris and Rouen, Gauguin joined his family in Copenhagen. He had no better luck as the agent of a French tarpaulin manufacturer, cocked a snook at the Danish art establishment, and quarrelled with his wife and relatives. In June 1885 he returned to France, finding refuge with a friend who lived on the coast at Dieppe. This picture was one of a number of seascapes painted during this period. It is Impressionist in technique, but far removed from the exuberance of comparable landscapes by Monet and others. The atmosphere is fresh but rather bleak, due mainly to the four huddled women on the beach; like many later figures in Gauguin's art, they seem preoccupied and indifferent to their surroundings.

▷ **Breton Shepherd Girl** 1886

Oil on canvas

IN THE SUMMER of 1886 Gauguin paid his first visit to Pont-Aven in Brittany, where he could 'board . . . for 60 francs a month'. However, cheap living was not his only motive. The province had always been somewhat isolated from the rest of France, retaining its distinctive customs and language into the 19th century. By the time Gauguin arrived, traditional dress was no longer worn except on special occasions, but at Pont-Aven the local people were obliging; Gauguin's imagination found enough to feed on and his taste for 'primitive' life was satisfied by clumping about in clogs on the cobbled streets. He also found congenial company at Pont-Aven, where the Pension Gloanec hosted a virtual artists' colony. In most of his work from this period Gauguin continued to be influenced by Impressionism, but *Breton Shepherd Girl* was not painted on the spot, Impressionist-fashion, but completed from a number of preparatory sketches. It shows Gauguin beginning to move towards a more patterned mode of picture-making.

◁ **Still Life with a Profile of Laval** 1886

Oil on canvas

THIS IS A BOLDLY effective painting, although it is one in which Gauguin is still digesting the various influences on his work. The arrangement and closely brushed treatment of the fruit recall a still life by Paul Cézanne, one of many works by still-unrecognized artists which Gauguin had purchased in the days of his prosperity. The way in which the man's head is abruptly cut off by the edge of the picture is a technique pioneered in Europe by Edgar Degas; by this date Gauguin would also have known of it through Japanese prints. The object behind the fruit is a pottery sculpture by Gauguin, and it is this that the man is studying so earnestly. He was Charles Laval, a 24-year-old artist whom Gauguin had recently met in Brittany. He became Gauguin's disciple and accompanied him to Martinique (page 15).

△ **St Pierre Bay, Martinique** 1887

Oil on canvas

'WHAT I WANT MOST of all is to flee Paris,' Gauguin wrote to his wife in March 1887. 'My reputation as an artist is growing day by day, but I sometimes go three days without eating, which undermines not only my health but my energy . . . I am off to Panama to live like a savage.' In April he left with Charles Laval (page 14). They were rapidly disillusioned, and worked as labourers to earn their fare to Martinique, 'a fine place where life is easy and cheap'. Life in Martinique proved anything but easy, and after coming down with malaria Gauguin worked his way back to France.

But the rich colours of the tropics had a permanent effect on his work. From this time onwards he would frequently reiterate his image of himself as a 'savage', and indulge in dreams of a tropical paradise free from the constraints of civilization.

◁ **Landscape at Pont-Aven** 1888

Oil on canvas

IN THE SUMMER of 1886 Gauguin paid his second visit to Brittany, which retained its appeal for him even after his experience of the lush, tropical landscape of Martinique. Quite apart from the picturesqueness of the Breton people and countryside, Pont-Aven was good for Gauguin's self-confidence: even in 1886 most of the younger painters at the Pension Gloanec had accepted the former 'Sunday painter' as their leader. In *Landscape at Pont-Aven* he has more or less broken with Impressionism, ignoring atmospheric effects and conventional perspective, so that the entire scene, rich and varied, presses forward towards the spectator. Nevertheless Gauguin's treatment of this and other landscapes was relatively naturalistic: his more radical experiments were reserved for figure paintings such as the extraordinary *Vision after the Sermon* (page 18).

▷ The Vision after the Sermon 1888

Oil on canvas

ALSO KNOWN AS *Jacob Wrestling with the Angel*. Having just heard a sermon on the subject, the women see it in a vision: that, Gauguin told Vincent van Gogh, was why the women were painted naturalistically while the rest of the scene was non-naturalistic. In actual fact Gauguin had been moving away from naturalism for some time, but the acceleration represented by the *Vision* was brought about through the influence of a younger artist, Emile Bernard. He and Gauguin developed a 'Synthetist' style which involved working from memory and imagination to eliminate inessentials, using bold outlines and areas of strong unbroken colour. Both men were also influenced by a literary and artistic movement, Symbolism, which encouraged a symbolic and rather cloudily 'spiritual' approach that surfaced in Gauguin's work from time to time over the years.

△ **Grape Harvest at Arles (Human Anguish)** 1888

Oil on canvas

GAUGUIN MET the Dutch painter Vincent van Gogh in 1886, and the two men often wrote to each other. In February 1888 van Gogh moved to Arles in the south of France, driven by a craving for a new life and more colourful climes that was not dissimilar to the impulse that had sent Gauguin to Martinique. At Arles van Gogh's art blossomed dramatically, but he was desperately lonely. He pressed Gauguin again and again to join him, and when van Gogh's brother Théo came up with the money, Gauguin consented. He arrived at van Gogh's 'Yellow House' on 23 October 1888, and began *Grape Harvest* about a week later. Demonstrating his new conviction that the artist should work from memory and imagination, Gauguin painted the picture indoors and included several Breton women in his 'southern' scene. Its original title was *Grape Harvest at Arles*, but Gauguin later renamed it *Human Anguish*, though there is no clear indication of what troubles the main figure. Possibly the implied subject is the same as that of *Loss of Virginity* (page 34).

▷ **Night Café at Arles** 1888

Oil on canvas

DURING THE TWO MONTHS he spent with van Gogh at Arles, Gauguin behaved as the master and van Gogh, desperate for company and less aggressively confident, accepted the role of admirer, if not disciple. He made a few experiments with Gauguin's Synthetist style, but it suited him no more than his immediate emotional responses and use of thick layers of paint (impasto) suited Gauguin. Nevertheless Gauguin's *Night Café at Arles* is an interesting effort in van Gogh's manner, using the sinister reds and greens with which van Gogh had expressed 'the terrible passions of humanity' when painting the same interior, the Café de la Gare. Van Gogh had also portrayed the proprietor, Mme Ginoux, here seated in the foreground. Thick blue smoke drifts across the café behind her, where three prostitutes, one with her hair in curlers, sit talking to the local postman, Roulin; both he and the Zouave soldier at the far left had also sat for van Gogh.

◁ **In the Garden at Arles** 1888

Oil on canvas

ALSO SOMETIMES KNOWN as *Old Women at Arles*. In this deeply impressive picture Gauguin has gone further still in the stylistic direction indicated by *The Vision after the Sermon* (page 18). Painted in mid-November 1888, early in Gauguin's stay at Arles with Vincent van Gogh, it was a response to a series of garden pictures by van Gogh which hung in Gauguin's room. Gauguin's clear intention was to show the superiority of painting from memory and imagination to painting from life, this being his current, Symbolist-influenced doctrine. The result here is a triumph of anti-naturalism. The absence of the horizon and indications of perspective creates a vertiginous feeling which is reinforced by the long sweeping diagonal running down the picture from left to right. All the forms are simplified, and the bush and fence, shutting in the procession of mournful women, emphasize the mysterious, claustrophobic atmosphere of the painting.

◁ **Les Alyscamps, Arles** 1888

Oil on canvas

LES ALYSCAMPS was a cypress-lined avenue, much frequented by Arlesians out for a stroll; van Gogh painted it several times. Although Gauguin's work is now far from his early Impressionism, this picture is more freely painted and closer to natural appearances than *In the Garden* (page 23). But he has injected into it a small note of unease and potential drama. The path runs beside a canal, where three women stand, faceless and still, like ghostly presences. In a different, jocular mood, Gauguin wrote to Théo van Gogh that the painting should be called *Three Graces at the Temple of Venus*. Théo, Vincent's brother, was supporting Gauguin, who paid him with a regular supply of canvases; the arrangement had been crucial in persuading Gauguin to leave for Arles and share a house with Vincent. But van Gogh and Gauguin proved to be temperamentally and artistically incompatible, and a few days after Christmas 1888 Gauguin left Arles for good.

△ **The Schuffenecker Family** 1889

Oil on canvas

ON HIS RETURN to Paris from Arles, Gauguin stayed for a time with the Schuffeneckers, painting this group portrait early in the year. He had known Emile Schuffenecker since the days when they had both been employed by the stockbroking firm of Bertin's. Schuffenecker too had given up business for art, although he made a more secure living than Gauguin as the drawing-master in a school. Gauguin several times took refuge with the Schuffeneckers when he was in difficulties, but his attitude to the helpful 'Schuff' tended to be condescending; he was more wary of Mme Schuffenecker, who resented his unsettling presence in their home. All this is reflected in the painting, where Emile is an ingratiating, almost suppliant figure in the background and the woman's voluminous coat and guardianship of the children emphasize her dominance. The setting is Schuffenecker's studio; the two pictures on the wall are a Japanese print and a still life by Gauguin.

▷ **La Belle Angèle** 1889

Oil on canvas

IN THE SPRING of 1889 Gauguin and several of his followers exhibited their work as 'the Impressionist and Synthetist Group' at the Café Volpini in Paris; in reality the show announced the arrival of a new, non-naturalistic school in reaction against Impressionism. Gauguin made some useful contacts at this time, but by June he was back in Brittany. Among his friends at Pont-Aven were the mayor and his wife Marie Angélique, whose portrait Gauguin set himself to paint. Shrewdly, he refused to let her see it until it was finished: when he presented it to her, she exclaimed 'Quelle horreur!' and told him to take it away. This has usually been interpreted as a sign of the Belle Angèle's conventional taste, but may well have had something to do with wounded vanity too! Gauguin achieved a striking effect by enclosing the woman in a medallion against a highly decorative background. The little idol is Peruvian, hinting at what Gauguin saw as his 'savage' origins and relating them to archaic Brittany.

▷ **The Yellow Christ** 1889

Oil on canvas

OVER A CENTURY after it was painted, this is still a vivid work of almost shocking force. Outlines are radically simplified and Gauguin has eliminated all but the minimum of detail needed to suggest the modelling of faces, figures and natural objects. The yellow Christ on the cross dominates the picture. It was based on a local crucifix, but Gauguin has enlarged it to life size, and it can be interpreted as a shrine, a vision, or even a here-and-now crucifixion; there was a strong tradition in European art of depicting the crucifixion surrounded by people in the dress of the painter's own time. The figure climbing over a wall is perhaps a reminder that, however soul-shaking the situation in the foreground, ordinary life goes on; this too was a common device in European art. A later Gauguin *Self-portrait with Yellow Christ* makes plain the resemblance between the Yellow Christ and the painter himself.

◁ **The Green Christ** 1889

Oil on canvas

LIKE *The Yellow Christ* (page 27), this can be regarded as a reworking of a traditional subject of Christian art: the deposition, or taking down of Christ's body from the cross by his grieving family and followers. Michelangelo, Rembrandt and many other great artists had created their own interpretations of the subject. Gauguin's deposition group was based on a wayside shrine at the village of Nizon, near Pont-Aven. Its forms needed relatively little simplification to fit in with his style, but its uniform green and strong sense of rhythm were Gauguin's contribution. The pose of the Breton woman in the foreground is absorbed into the rhythm, bringing the worlds of miracle and everyday into contact. Even more than in *The Yellow Christ,* the background – a seaweed gatherer at work, cattle grazing, a ship on the horizon – set the scene in contemporary Brittany.

△ **Christ in the Garden of Olives** 1889

Oil on canvas

THE MOST DARING of Gauguin's 'religious' paintings of 1889, unmistakably a self-portrait. Traditionally, the Garden of Olives was where Jesus spent the night preparing himself for his destiny. In Gauguin's interpretation, the master is being abandoned by his disciples, completing his isolation. The sombre trees and close-hatched brushwork envelope the lonely figure; only his extraordinary, flaming hair prevents his slumped form from conveying total despair. If Gauguin's self-identification with Christ seems pretentious, it should be said that the idea of the artist as messiah and martyr was very much in the air during this period.

◁ **Bonjour,
Monsieur Gauguin** 1889

Oil on canvas

IN SEPTEMBER 1889, feeling that
Pont-Aven was becoming too
popular and losing its authentic
atmosphere, Gauguin moved to
the more remote hamlet of Le
Pouldu, close to the sea. There
he painted *The Green Christ*
(page 28) and *Christ in the
Garden of Olives* (page 29),
which manifested his self-
identification with Jesus.
Bonjour, Monsieur Gauguin is
more replete with ironies. Late
in 1888, Gauguin and van
Gogh had visited Montpellier
and looked at *Bonjour, Monsieur
Courbet,* a splendid if self-
congratulatory self-portrait by
the Realist painter Gustave
Courbet; it showed Courbet as
a genial summer-time hiker,
being greeted respectfully by
his patron and a servant. By
contrast, Gauguin shows
himself muffled up in greatcoat
and cape against the Breton
winter, and with no one to
greet him; the woman appears
to be facing the artist, but her
feet are leading her off to the
right. However, the mood of
the picture is far from
despairing.

△ **The Seaweed Harvest** 1889

Oil on canvas

IN ITS SUPERB CLARITY, this represents the culmination of one side of Gauguin's art, with its broad contours, simplified shapes and regular brushstrokes creating an effect of patterning and flatness. In the not very distant future Gauguin would modify this technique, making it more subtle, and dramatic croppings at the edges of his compositions would also become less common. *The Seaweed Harvest* was painted in December 1889 at Le Pouldu, where Gauguin spent most of the winter. He described the picture in a letter to van Gogh (the two men were still friends, despite the events at Arles), and also the life of the women gathering the seaweed for fertilizer. Perhaps playing up to van Gogh's interest in social questions, he described the way in which they worked, without adequate clothing, in the biting cold, and reflected on the struggle for existence and 'the harsh law of nature'. The main indication of such awareness is confined to the enlarged, raw-looking hands of the foreground figure.

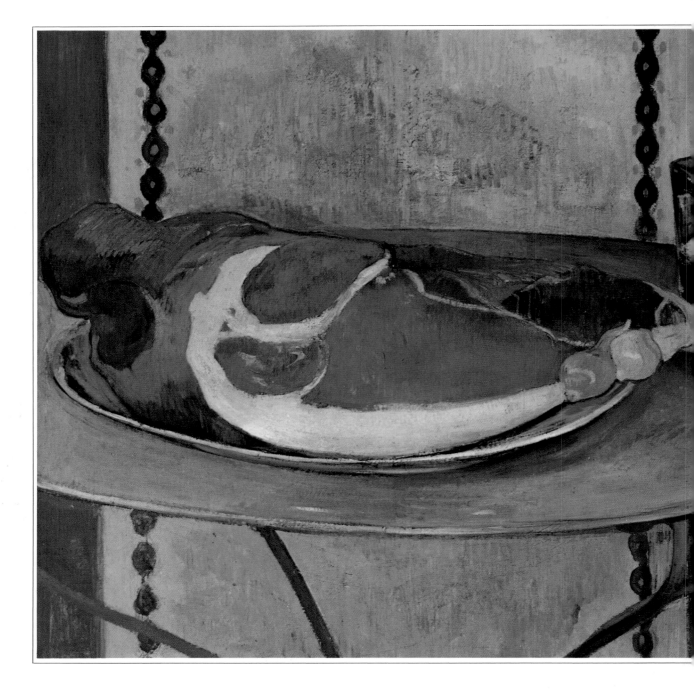

◁ **Still Life with Ham** 1889

Oil on canvas

THIS APPARENTLY modest little canvas is a fine example of Gauguin's skill as a still-life painter. He often produced still life or included still-life groups in his figure paintings, using objects such as idols or ceramics to emphasize a mood.

Here, however, he has taken a few simple items – a joint of ham, some small onions, a half-filled glass of red wine – and painted them as an apparently unarranged group. Closer examination reveals how carefully the picture has in fact been composed to balance the elliptical table-top, its curved supports and the verticals of the wallpaper pattern behind them. There is also an interesting tension between the solid objects on the table, conveying a sense of depth, and the flat immediacy of the wallpaper, one curious result being that the table might almost be suspended by what look like chains but are actually vertical lines of beading on the wallpaper.

▷ **Loss of Virginity** 1891

Oil on canvas

ALSO KNOWN as *The Awakening of Spring*. It was painted when Gauguin was mixing with Symbolist poets such as Jean Moréas and Stéphane Mallarmé, and receiving great encouragement from them. This seems to account for the programmatic nature of the work, with its rather heavy-handed visual clues (the lascivious fox, the plucked, scarlet-tipped flower). The arbitrarily coloured Breton background and the procession in the distance remain unexplained. The model was Gauguin's mistress, Juliette Huet. By early 1891 the painter had decided against Madagascar because it was too close to civilization, and had opted for Tahiti. He raised 9,000 francs by selling 30 paintings at the Hôtel Drouet, paid a rapid final visit to his wife and family in Copenhagen, and left Marseilles for his savage paradise on 1 April 1891.

◁ **Women on a Beach** 1891

Oil on canvas

HAVING CONVINCED the government that he was visiting Tahiti on an 'artistic mission', Gauguin was able to travel on a cut-price ticket via Melbourne, Sidney and Noumea, arriving at Papeete on 8 June 1891. Quickly disillusioned with the town, he went to live among the natives at Mataiea, where he rented a bamboo hut. *Women on a Beach* was one of the earliest of his serious studies of island life; he was evidently pleased with it, making a second version the following year in which the woman's missionary-issue dress is replaced by the traditional and more revealing pareu. The model for one or possibly both women was probably Gauguin's thirteen-year-old *vahine*, Teha'amana. The figures are unusually monumental for Gauguin, but the background retains the flat, clearly demarcated, strip-like character he so often favoured.

△ **The Meal** 1891

Oil on canvas

ALSO KNOWN SIMPLY AS *Bananas;* the splendid red hand of bananas was obviously a motif that pleased Gauguin, who used it in several other pictures. This one began as a pure still life, its exotic fruits contrasting nicely with the meat, onions and wine of the European repast in *The Ham* (page 33); the large bowl and knife are a kind of homage to Cézanne's *Still Life with Fruit Bowl, Glass and Apples*, which Gauguin had owned and admired intensely. By adding the three solemn children in their curiously modern clothes, Gauguin changed the mood of the painting, giving it a sense of watchful waiting that is certainly not just that of greedy, impatient children. As in a number of European paintings from Titian to Manet, the view through the open door adds to the quality of mysteriousness that Gauguin sought.

▷ **The Man with the Axe** 1891

Oil on canvas

WOMEN DOMINATE Gauguin's pictorial account of Tahiti, so it comes as a surprise to find this dynamic male figure swinging his axe at some object beyond the picture plane. The canvas was painted early in Gauguin's stay at Mataeia, but was based on a scene he had observed earlier. It obviously had great significance for him, since he described it at some length, though in rather obscure terms replete with references to Polynesian and Indian religion. He seems to have had in mind some kind of spiritual synthesis, and this may be reflected in the borrowings and mixings which are particularly evident here. The man's posture is taken from a figure on the Parthenon frieze; 'he' is in fact rather sexually ambiguous; and the styles within the picture range from schematization and expressive use of colour to naturalism – which is, oddly, most marked in the background, where the boat sails close to the shore, inside the line of the breakers.

◁ **Vairaoumati tei oa (Her name is Vairaoumati)** 1892

Oil on canvas

THIS WAS PAINTED in about March 1892, and is one of the earliest surviving Tahitian nudes by Gauguin. Vairaoumati was a mortal maiden seduced by the king of the Tahitian gods, Oro, whom Gauguin shows standing behind her. She bore the god a child, who became the ancestor of the Areoi, a privileged Tahitian caste whose sexual behaviour was not subject to any restrictions. Freedom from restraint – and guilt – was very much the image of the 'South Seas' that attracted Gauguin and other westerners. He has pictured Vairaoumati like a figure from an ancient Egyptian painting, with her head in profile and her torso turned to the front. In one version of the painting Vairaoumati is holding a piece of fruit, but here an impulse of mockery has prompted Gauguin to put a cigarette between her fingers.

The House of Song (Te Fare Hymenee) 1892

Oil on canvas

▷ *Overleaf pages 42-43*

PAINTED ON VERY COARSE canvas, which is partly responsible for the picture's distinctive quality; according to Gauguin himself, it dates from before the end of April 1892. The soft, blurred forms and subdued, firelit atmosphere are unusual in Gauguin's work, but wholly appropriate to the subject, which is the communal house where the Tahitians gathered to gossip and sing. In his book *Noa Noa*, Gauguin described how they started with a prayer, recited by an old man and then chanted by everyone present as a refrain; then the session of singing, joking and storytelling began. For once, Gauguin is evidently not myth-making, since he shows the islanders in the more or less European-style clothes which they were increasingly adopting. The poses of his more distinctly outlined female figures are closely related to those in other paintings, notably *Women on a Beach* (page 37) and *When Will You Marry?* (page 45).

◁ **Vahine no te vi** 1892

Oil on canvas

'EVERYTHING IN THE landscape blinded and dazzled me,' Gauguin wrote of his first few months in Tahiti, and he undertook a number of stylistic experiments before finding the way of representing the island and its people that suited him best. *Vahine no te vi* is one of Gauguin's least characteristic paintings. There are few parallels in his art to the girl's emphatically turning pose and the sculpturesque treatment of the drapery of her dress. However, the number of images of fully (western) clothed Tahitians in his early work probably signifies only that he was still responding to the realities of island life: under pressure from the missionaries, and in imitation of their European masters, the Tahitians were rapidly abandoning the simple pareu for a more 'civilized' garb. Soon, Gauguin would sink into his dream of a Tahitian paradise, and European dress would become a rarity in his work.

▷ When Will You Marry? 1892

Oil on canvas

IN MAY 1892 Gauguin wrote to his wife telling her that he had at last settled down and grasped something of the real character of the Tahitians, 'whom I represent in a very enigmatic manner'. The enigma was compounded by the Tahitian titles he gave his works (implying a mastery of the native language that he never achieved), which were usually not much more informative when translated into French. *Nafea faa ipoipo?* – When will you marry? – has at least some relationship to the picture, since one girl is wearing a magnolia behind her ear to indicate that she is looking for a husband. The picture itself is stunningly bold and original. Horizontal bands of colour run across the canvas in an almost schematized fashion, broken by the monumental central group with its contrasts of brown, red, pink and orange. The arrangement of the overlapping figures is both psychologically uneasy and fascinating.

▷ **Arearea (Joyousness)** 1892

Oil on canvas

A PASTORAL VISION of Tahiti as Gauguin had hoped it would be, and as it perhaps sometimes seemed. Two girls sit beneath a tree beside a lagoon; one plays the flute. In the background, worshippers pay their devotions before a carving of a Polynesian god: the scene is almost certainly a figment of Gauguin's imagination, since the old customs had been thoroughly suppressed. The almost flat, non-naturalistic colours, still very striking, created much unfavourable comment in 1893, when Gauguin's Tahitian work was exhibited in Paris by the dealer Durand-Ruel. The red dog became particularly notorious, and when a journalist interviewed Gauguin in 1895 he called his article 'Orange Rivers and Red Dogs'. Like many an artist since, Gauguin had to explain that his use of colour was intentional and calculated, 'a sort of music, if you like. I create, by the arrangement of lines and colours, using as a pretext some subject drawn from nature or life, symphonies, harmonies.'

◁ **By the Sea** 1892

Oil on canvas

THIS KIND OF VIGOROUS physical action is rare in Gauguin's work. Here it is combined with brilliant decorative effects in one of the artist's most colourful and joyous creations. A girl plunges naked into the water while her companion finishes undressing; neither seems troubled by the presence of the fisherman. The writhing, almost organic quality of the sand, tropical blossoms and tree remind us that this was painted in the 1890s, when the curvilinear Art Nouveau style was establishing itself. The sinuosities of Art Nouveau had an undisguised erotic appeal, which here underlines the implied sexual liberation of the women. Both Biblical and mythological bathing scenes had long been used in western art as an excuse for erotic titillation, and to the buttoned-up 19th century the physical freedom and energy of Gauguin's women would have carried its own message. Typically, Gauguin excludes any hint of sentimentality or coyness from the scene.

▷ **What! Are You Jealous?** 1892

Oil on canvas

THIS IS ANOTHER of the enigmatic titles that Gauguin was so fond of, provoking endless speculation among commentators. If it has any relevance at all, it probably implies some kind of competition between the two women. It is likely that Gauguin, with his self-confessed love of 'mysteriousness', had no definite situation in mind; and he always insisted that the proper titles for works of this sort were the Tahitian ones he gave them – in this case, *Aha oe feii?* All the same, knowing the English equivalent alters one's response to the picture and makes it hard to believe that there is not a certain tension in the scene – 'trouble in paradise'. It could easily be interpreted as a sequel to the exuberance of *By the Sea* (page 49). As always, Gauguin's sources were as much art-historical as ethnic, and the central figure is actually taken from a reproduction of a frieze on the Theatre of Dionysus in Athens.

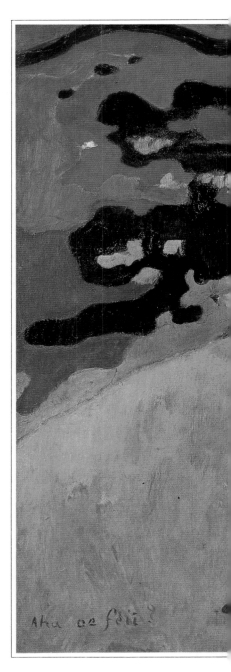

◁ **The Spirit of the Dead Keeps Watch** 1892

Oil on canvas

ONE ACCOUNT BY GAUGUIN of the genesis of this work, *Manao tupapau,* is that he came home late at night from Papeete to find his young *vahine,* Teha'amana, lying face down on the bed, rigid with terror. Gauguin was infected by her fear, and taken aback by the feeling that she was a strange being whom he had never really known. The story seems to be indebted to Edgar Allan Poe, whom Gauguin admired; it is just as likely that the picture was suggested by his reading, the main source of his knowledge of traditional Tahitian beliefs, most of which were dying or dead. The scene is shown as the girl understands it, with the figure of a *tupapau,* or spirit of the dead, behind her, and its phosphorescent flowers sparking in the room. On a slightly different level, the painting is a brilliant colour symphony and the girl a nude intended to challenge comparison with masterworks of the European tradition such as Manet's *Olympia.*

◁ Hina Tefatou (The Moon and the Earth) 1893

Oil on canvas

IN SEARCH OF the mysterious, Gauguin was enchanted by Polynesian mythology. In his writings he claimed to have heard many stories from the lips of his native wife, Teha'amana, but most of his information actually came from a book, Moeranhout's *Voyages,* based on investigations made half a century earlier, before Tahitian culture had started to disappear under the pressure of the European presence. Here Gauguin visualized Hina, the moon goddess, pleading with her son Fatu, god of the Earth, to grant immortality to the human race. Fatu refused: 'The earth shall die, the vegetation shall die, it shall die like the human beings who feed upon it.' The monumental, modelled figures of the gods dominate the beautiful, decoratively patterned landscape.

▷ **Ea haere ia oe? (Where Are You Going?)** 1893

Oil on canvas

THE TITLES OF GAUGUIN'S canvases were generally intended to be suggestive rather than precisely descriptive. All the same, it is tempting to link this one with his decision to return to France. For all his delight in the island's atmosphere and his self-image as a 'savage' who was being purged of civilized attitudes, Gauguin was often lonely without the friends whom he had hoped would join him and set up an artistic colony in the tropics. He was also miserably poor, finding that money due from France was liable to be forwarded, if at all, without any great sense of urgency. He also experienced an upsurge of ambition, knowing that he could bring back with him dozens of superb canvases which ought to take Paris by storm. In this painting, the huge, luscious fruit and the woman's breast suggest the pleasures Gauguin would be sacrificing if he went; and the background too emphasizes the warm, rich, natural life of Tahiti.

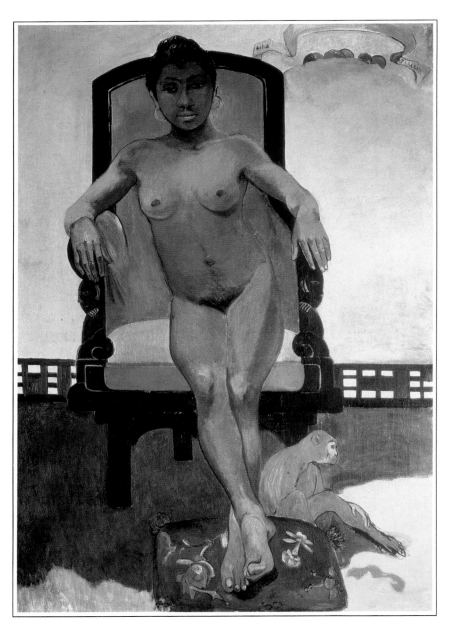

◁ **Annah the Javanese** 1893

Oil on canvas

ON HIS RETURN to Paris from Tahiti, Gauguin moved into a studio lent to him by the poster artist Alphonse Mucha, and embarked on a vigorous campaign of self-promotion. In November 1893 he held his first major one-man show at the Durand-Ruel Gallery; but although his Tahitian paintings and sculptures caused a stir, he sold only 11 canvases. In December he was introduced to Annah, who became (in one order or another) his maid, model and mistress. She was actually of Indian-Malayan origin, but Gauguin preferred to believe that she was Javanese, since he had admired Java's culture ever since his visit to the Paris Exhibition of 1889, and modelled some of his Tahitian figures on sculptures from the great Buddhist shrine of Borobudur. For a few months Gauguin and Annah, both dressed with colourful eccentricity, were prominent in the artistic bohemias of Paris and Brittany.

▷ **Self-portrait with a Hat** 1893-4

Oil on canvas

LIKE MANY ARTISTS of his generation – the Post-Impressionists – Gauguin was obsessed with his own image, which he painted, drew and carved over 40 times. On several occasions he represented himself as a martyr, for example in *Christ in the Garden of Olives* (1889, page 29) and seven years later in *Self-portrait near Golgotha*. Here, not long returned from Tahiti, he resembles a carved idol, with his face powerfully modelled in highlighted planes. The painting was done from a mirror, so that behind him *The Spirits of the Dead Keep Watch* (page 53) appears as a reversed image. The setting is his Paris studio in the rue Vercingétorix, which he was able to rent in December 1893, after receiving a windfall inheritance, and decorated in colourful 'South Seas' style.

> **Village under Snow** 1894

Oil on canvas

THIS PICTURE is a curious throwback to Gauguin's early style, using the small, swiftly applied brushstrokes with which the Impressionists attempted to capture the atmosphere of a scene. However, by comparison with *Snow Scene* (page 10) the strongly drawn contours and monumental design are those of the mature artist. Though reminiscent of Brittany, the canvas was probably painted early in 1894, before Gauguin revisited his former rural haunts – which, paradoxically, he represented with almost tropical warmth. However, any nostalgia Gauguin may have felt was qualified by the disastrous nature of his trip to the province. His former landlady at Le Pouldu refused to return the works he had left with her, and a court upheld her refusal (Gauguin had left owing her money). During a brawl at Concarneau the painter broke his leg just above the ankle. And having allowed Annah the Javanese to return to Paris ahead of him, he arrived to find that she had cleared out his studio and disappeared, leaving nothing of value – except his 'worthless' canvases.

◁ **Mahana no atua
(The Day of the God)** 1894

Oil on canvas

THIS SMALL PICTURE has long been one of Gauguin's most popular works. It was not painted in Tahiti but in France, between his first and second visits to the island. Though it purports to be a scene of Tahitian ritual, it actually represents Gauguin's purely imaginative response to his reading and experiences; in particular, the god is a composite of Easter Island and Javanese images. The composition is divided into three main 'friezes' which reinforce its hieratic quality: the god and his devotees; the symmetrical group of bathers; and the extraordinary water in the foreground, its lovely pattern of 'reflections' anticipating the development of pure abstraction in painting. During this period Gauguin was working on the materials for his books *Ancien Culte Mahorie* and *Noa Noa,* which he hoped would help the general public to understand his Tahitian works.

▷ Nave Nave Mahana
(Days of Delight) 1896

Oil on canvas

THIS IS ONE of Gauguin's most idyllic pictures of Tahitian life, a crowded but beautifully composed scene in which every part of the canvas is vividly alive. The soft colours harmonize, with none of the bold contrast found elsewhere in Gauguin's work. A great deal seems to be going on, yet the impression is of a silent moment, stolen out of time. The separation between the life and the work of an artist has rarely been wider than in Gauguin's case. He left France in June 1895, not so much because he longed for Tahiti as because he despaired of establishing himself in his native land – and perhaps, too, because he wished at least to maintain the legend that had grown up around him. But he was now a sick man, frequently hospitalized, still desperately poor, and yet capable of creating the tranquil beauty of *Nave Nave Mahana*.

NAVE NAVE MAHANA
P. Gauguin 1896

△ **Te Arii Vahine (The Noble Woman)** 1896

Oil on canvas

EARLY IN 1896 Gauguin was in pain from his broken ankle and had developed sores on his legs; although he was not aware of it, he was suffering from a syphilitic infection that prevented his ankle from healing. Yet in April he wrote cheerfully to his close friend Daniel de Monfreid describing a large picture he had just completed: 'a naked queen lying on a green carpet, a servant picking fruit, two old men . . . I don't think I have ever done anything in colour with such a deep, resonant quality.' The composition is divided diagonally into two areas, one occupied by the reclining woman, the other filled with a superbly decorative mass of flowering trees. The serpent twined round the tree trunk suggests that the 'queen' is a Tahitian Eve.

△ **Christmas Night** 1896?

Oil on canvas

ALSO KNOWN AS *The Blessing of the Oxen*. This canvas and *Village under Snow* (page 58) were among Gauguin's possessions when he died in the Marquesas. The basic scene in *Village under Snow* reappears in the background here, though executed in a smoother style which lends credence to the theory that *Christmas Night* was painted later, after Gauguin's return to Tahiti. It has also been pointed out that the women's faces look more Polynesian than Breton; but this is not a decisive consideration, since Gauguin was perfectly capable of deliberate cultural cross-referencing, irrespective of the models in front of him. The object on the right is a wayside shrine with a nativity very much in the Breton style (compare it with the deposition in *The Green Christ*, page 28). Cattle have traditionally been allotted a humble but significant role in nativity scenes, so there can be little doubt that Gauguin intends the picture to transcend the division between past and present, making Breton cattle witnesses of the Gospel nativity.

Nevermore 1897

Oil on canvas

▷ *Overleaf pages 66-67*

THE MOST CELEBRATED of all Gauguin's Tahitian nudes, *Nevermore* is similar in subject to *The Spirit of the Dead Keeps Watch* (page 53) in showing a fearful girl, turned away from what she believes to be a spirit, embodied in the raven on the windowsill. The raven and the picture's title are direct references to the poem by Edgar Allan Poe, with its sinister refrain 'Quoth the Raven, "Nevermore".' Gauguin wrote his own description of *Nevermore*: 'I wanted to suggest, with a simple nude, a certain long-vanished barbaric luxury. The whole thing is saturated with colours that are sombre and sad . . . As a title, *Nevermore;* not exactly the raven of Edgar Poe, but the bird of the devil who keeps watch . . . I think it is a good canvas.'

△ Where Do We Come From? Who Are We? Where Are We Going? 1897

Oil on canvas

THIS IS THE LARGEST and most ambitious canvas Gauguin ever painted, and was intended as his final statement. Ill, in debt and depressed by the death of his favourite child, Aline, he worked feverishly, day and night, through December 1897, painting straight on to the canvas without making preparatory sketches or using

models. Then he swallowed a quantity of arsenic, only to throw it up straight away and live. That, at any rate, was Gauguin's account of how the work came to be painted, given in a letter to his friend Daniel de Monfreid in February 1898. At least some elements in the story were fabricated to embellish the Gauguin legend, since he did in fact make detailed preparatory sketches which still exist. Completing this great work gave him new hope, and he had it shipped to France, urging Monfreid to give it the maximum public exposure. The title, too, seems very much calculated to appeal to the European sensibility. The painting is meant to be 'read' from right to left, depicting the cycle of life from birth to extreme old age.

▽ **Faa Iheihe** 1898

Oil on canvas

ALSO KNOWN AS *Tahitian Pastoral* and *Preparations for a Festival.* The warm red-yellow tones and softened forms of this painting make it one of Gauguin's most joyful productions, presenting an extraordinary contrast to the blue-green sobriety of *Where Do We Come From?* (page 68). The dream-like atmosphere is very strong, with the figures apparently on the point of drifting upwards in a red-gold mist. In *Where Do We*

Come From? many of the figures are taken over from Gauguin's earlier works, as part of a grand life-summary; here, the poses are new, adding to the sense of a fresh beginning. Simple equations between life and art are always dangerous, but it is nevertheless true that Gauguin's prospects seemed to be improving during 1898, perhaps renewing his vision of Tahiti as at least a potential paradise.

◁ Three Tahitians 1899

Oil on canvas

THE DATE ON THIS CANVAS has sometimes been read as '97' rather than '99'; however, the unusually space-filling, solid figures are akin to those in the *Maternity* paintings of 1899 by Gauguin, which tends to support the most common reading. The composition is audacious but wholly successful, with two figures seen from behind and the face of the central figure – a man – almost completely hidden from the spectator. As so often in Gauguin's Tahitian works, there is a sense of secrecy and whispered confidences; he himself noted that although life on the island was lived in the open, it was 'intimate all the same, among the thickets and secluded brooks, where women whisper in an immense palace dressed by nature herself'. For all his 'savage' posturing and native 'wives', Gauguin, like other Europeans, felt on occasion that the Tahitians lived in a world that he could never enter.

△ Sunflowers 1901

Oil on canvas

IN 1895 GAUGUIN asked his faithful friend Daniel de Monfreid to send him some flower seeds for his garden. Monfreid, as usual, obliged. Among the seeds were sunflowers, which flourished in the Tahitian climate; and the blooms in this fine still life were their descendants. On one level the painting is almost certainly a reminiscence of Vincent van Gogh. At Arles, in 1888, Gauguin had executed a highly effective, vertiginous portrait of van Gogh at work on one of his sunflower paintings. In 1901, just before leaving Tahiti for the Marquesas, Gauguin painted a number of still lifes including four sunflower studies. This one has a distinctly Symbolist flavour, with a mysterious eye staring out of a flower-head at the back.

▷ **And the Gold of their Bodies** 1901

Oil on canvas

IN AUGUST 1901 Gauguin sold his Tahitian property, and a month later embarked for the Marquesas. There he hoped to find the unspoiled Eden that eluded him and, on a more practical note, a place where the living was cheaper and easier than Tahiti; as he was now receiving fairly regular payments from Europe, his prospects seemed better than for some years. On 16 September he landed at Atuana on the island of Hiva Oa (Dominique), and within a few weeks he had purchased land in the village and built a hut. Gauguin's delight in his new surroundings is patent in *And the Gold of their Bodies*, with its large, calm forms and marshalled brushstrokes. Significantly, he no longer practised mystification by giving his paintings Polynesian titles, and his final period is marked by a new freedom and simplicity.

△ **Riders on the Beach** 1902

Oil on canvas

IN THE MARQUESAS Gauguin found a rather surprising new subject in scenes with horses and riders. In *The Ford* (1901), a group of riders crosses a stream on their way to the beach; the painting shown here is like the next episode in the 'story', in which the riders have come out on to the beach; and another painting of 1902 (now in the Folkwang Museum, Essen) shows what appears to be the same party, but this time from behind, riding away from the spectator along the sand. Two of the men wear European-style trousers, but the leaders are dressed in tunics with mysterious hoods, rather like the spirit of the dead on page 53; if they really are spirits, the painting takes on an unexpected meaning, perhaps as a kind of Polynesian Dance of Death. Stylistically it is very much a tribute to Edgar Degas' racecourse scenes.

▷ **Contes Barbares** 1902

Oil on canvas

HERE GAUGUIN has momentarily reverted to the habit of giving enigmatic titles to his works, this time in French. The most likely explanation of the scene is that the girls are telling 'barbaric tales' of the ancient Polynesian gods, and that the intrusive, diabolic figure with the claw feet represents the corrupting influence of the West. Both girls' poses are derived from the sculpted frieze at Borobudur in Java, of which Gauguin possessed photographs; the central figure's 'lotus position' is of course well known. Most oddly of all, the man is a portrait of Jacob Meyer de Haan, a Dutch painter who had become a follower of Gauguin and had worked with him in Brittany in 1889. Gauguin had painted him in satanic guise at the time, and here, though de Haan was long dead (1895), resurrects his baleful image.

◁ **Girl with a Fan** 1902

Oil on canvas

SOME MARQUESAN WOMEN were red-haired, and Gauguin particularly admired one named Tohotaua; she is the girl with the fan here, and also the kneeling girl in *Contes Barbares* (page 76). The portrait was painted from a photograph which was found among the artist's possessions after his death. It shows the many small changes he made to turn it into a work of art, including the view from above which gives the chair an appropriate presence in the picture. Above all, in the photograph Tohotaua's breasts are covered, but Gauguin has given her back the physical freedom taken away by the missionaries. Paradoxically, it was in the more remote Marquesas that Gauguin's sexual non-conformity and contempt for officialdom caused him most difficulties – mainly, it must be admitted, self-created; he was still in the toils when he died on 8 May 1903.

ACKNOWLEDGEMENTS

The Publisher would like to thank the following for their kind permission to reproduce the paintings in this book:

Musée des Beaux-Arts de Lyon, 62-63; **Musée d'Orsay Paris** © **Photo R.M.N** 25-26; **Scottish National Gallery of Modern Art** 72; **Tate Gallery, London** 70-71.

Bridgeman Art Library, London /**Albright Knox Art Gallery, Buffalo, New York** 27, 52-53; /**Art Institute of Chicago, USA** 22-23, 60-61; /**Baltimore Museum of Art, Maryland, USA** 44; /**Boston Museum of Fine Arts, Mass.** 68-69; /**Carlsberg Collection, Copenhagen** 15; /**Ny Carlsberg Glyptotek, Copenhagen** 8; /**Chrysler Museum, Norfolk, Virginia** 34-35; /**Collection Hahnloser, Bern** 56: /**Collection Josefowitz, New York;** 14 /**Courtauld Institute Galleries, University of London** 66-67; /**Giraudon/Musée d'Orsay, Paris** 24, 57, 36-37, 74-75; /**Hermitage, St Petersburg** 55, 73; /**Laing Art Gallery, Newcastle-upon-Tyne** 12-13; /**Louvre, Paris** 38, 46-47, 58-59; /**Musées Royaux des Beaux-Arts de Belgique, Brussels** 28: /**Museum Folkwang, Essen, Germany** 31, 77, 78; /**Museum of Modern Art, New York** 54; /**Narodni Gallery, Prague** 30; /**National Gallery of Art, Washington DC** 48-49; /**National Gallery of Scotland, Edinburgh** 18-19, /**Norton Gallery, Palm Beach** 29; /**Ordrupgaard, Copenhagen** 20; /**Phillips Collection, Washington DC** 32-33; /**Private Collection** 10,11,16-17, 39, 42-43, 45, 65, 76; /**Pushkin Museum, Moscow** 21, 40, 50-51, 64.